FINISHING LINE PRESS

www.finishinglinepress.com

# With My Sister, in a Tornado Warning

*poems by*

## Shellie Harwood

*Finishing Line Press*
Georgetown, Kentucky

*I came to explore the wreck.*
*The words are purposes.*
*The words are maps.*
*I came to see the damage that was done*
*and the treasures that prevail.*

*—Adrienne Rich, "Diving into the Wreck"*

# With My Sister, in a Tornado Warning

*For Allen, who is refuge.*

## ACKNOWLEDGMENTS

Thank you to the editors of the following journals, in which the poems in
this book first appeared.

*Ember Days*: "Lady Ablaze"
*Mudfish 22*: "When She Runs"
*Oberon Poetry/* 18th Annual Issue/ 2020: "With My Sister, In a Tornado
Warning"
*Sixfold Summer 2020*: "With My Sister, in a Tornado Warning;" "Last Train
to New Haven;" "On the Line;" "Early Evening, Late September;" "Virus"

A big thanks to my friends and family, for reading and embracing my poetry
and plays through the years.
Thanks to my daughter, Morgan, and my son, Nick, for their constant
encouragement, and to Peder Aresvik, for his striking photo on the book's
cover.
And, finally, a special thank you to my husband, Allen, for his unwavering
support, and his patience with my moods and fits of inspiration.

Publisher: Leah Huete de Maines
Editor: Christen Kincaid
Cover Art: Peder Aresvik
Author Photo: Allen Grunerud
Cover Design: Elizabeth Maines McCleavy

Order online: www.finishinglinepress.com
        also available on amazon.com

Author inquiries and mail orders:
Finishing Line Press
PO Box 1626
Georgetown, Kentucky 40324
USA

# Table of Contents

**I Bend Close to Examine the Photo "A Woman Hitting a Neo-Nazi with Her Handbag"**

You seem to snarl, Danuta. In the town square in Växjö, Sweden, circa 1985.
You wear no-nonsense shoes, a man's baggy jacket,
your pleated skirt balloons. You belong in a photograph of a housewife
sternly dragging sullen children home from a schoolyard.
Yet, here you are, flying through the square like a banshee,
or Saint Joan. Launched at a Neo-Nazi marcher, your handbag frozen
in mid-air, a split-second above his shaved and branded head.
Bruegel may have painted you at some point, placed you in a corner
wearing that hell-hath-no-fury face, brandishing a torch, a chiseled spoon.

They said no to your statue in the public square, Danuta.
No to your mother limping out of Auschwitz.
No to your big calves, your big anger.
No to your madness, your leap later from the Växjö water tower.
And, no, because God knows before your flight of fury no hands ever
molded monuments to glorify the anguished cry of *enough is still enough*.

Before today, I did not own a handbag.
Not even a ruched satin clutch with a pearly clasp to hold my MetroCard and
the Oh-So-Fine-Wine lipstick that get me where it is I'm going.
I move unencumbered; weapons slow me down.

But, here now, tags cut free from a sturdy strap slung on my shoulder,
I wait in the square for the vast parade
of the very fine people.
I have set your expression on my own face, Danuta,
have weighted my bag with broken stones from toppled statues.
I will swing it wide, for you.

## When She Runs

At six,
her laces trail behind her
when she runs

moving like serpents
round her feet on the blacktop
waiting to pull her down

I call her back to me
to tie and twist the double knots again
before the bell has rung

She will not shelter in her place
when first the bullets come
she will fly frantic
laces undone

I beg you
watch for her
and give her cover

Cup your hands over her ears
to mute the guns

How will you know which one to save?
How will you know her?

She'll be the one
head back
teeth bared
breast heaving

She'll wear no armor
no metal jacket

Her laces trail behind her
when she runs

## With My Sister, In a Tornado Warning

You offer me wine, when I come to you.
Red or white. As if today it could matter.

You are the perfect hostess.
Even under a tornado warning, even when
your lip is split and bulging
like a bulb
too late for planting.
Red, I say.

Your face blooms from his hand:
fuchsia, violets, O'Keefe's dark iris,
an explosion of forget-me-nots.

I think of the photo I have
of your wedding in Carmel-by-the-Sea.
He is dipping you back, with only one hand,
in your satin. Your dark hair raking the sand.
His smile says, *look what I can do.*

My glass empty, I stare out your window.
Sky is blackening above your sunflowers.
It may be time.

First, I must stitch you up;
thread the needle's eye and
sew shut every opening: the eyes, the mouth, the heart,
the vulva. Taking care not to puncture,
before I bite the thread and tie the knot.

Then we sit, fists in our throats,
hands grasped across the rough wooden table,
splinters digging through.

Out over your garden, a funnel cloud is forming.

We are in no hurry.
You are sewn shut.
Nothing, now, will ever get in.

3

## Pompeii

*For my grandfather*

In this kitchen the old man allowed the yeast to proof into
a creamy foam, mixed and kneaded, punched with knotted

fingers, floured the air and dough. Say you were a hungry
child, and this man baked that yearning into shining loaves,

lifting you high on a wobbly stool to cut out biscuits with a
drinking glass. Say, when his heart buzzed, stopped like a

timer under his starched dress shirt, with his London tie with
the Big Ben on, that he fell like a city in his white apron,

flour poofing up in clouds as he hit the floor. And say the child
climbed over the chalk outlining his body, melted into him,

forever fused, mouth circled open in the shape of his name.
Say you stayed there while the dough kept rising, up over the

pans, like lava, over the counter, bubbling down the cupboards
and across the floor. Say you were preserved down there, petrified

in floury ash, curled around the old man in the space between the love
and loss,
like in old Pompeii.

**Motion**

as a child
my mother raced an invisible horse
through Wyoming sagebrush
whipping its flanks for speed
to bruises
forgetting they were her own

grew with weeds
forgotten
in unsettled spaces
shredded by wind

jostled in dirty trains
back and forth
on a warped rail
that separated her father from her mother
        mouth full of dust
in her mind
sent away
never for

like to have seen her racing
that girl
who keeps me at arm's length
whip in hand
who will not move or be moved
trusting neither love nor motion

## Last Train to New Haven

As doors slide shut, he slips through
onto the half-deserted train.

No more than a boy,
carrying the weight of a starving sparrow.
A shirt of magenta, flowered
in periwinkle blue.
Head down, hands empty,
wanting only safe passage home.

A pack of them, hyenas, laughing
as he moves, hunted, down
the lurching aisle.
*Kiss, kiss. Isn't she a pretty one?*
A boot out, then, or a sneaker in front of him
in his path, tangling his slender legs.

I see it fast-motion:
boy flying, broken metal seat arm rising
up to him.
*Faggot* hissing in the air
as the pack of them scatter, screeching,
to another car.

I have nothing. Half-empty bottle of
Poland Spring,
napkins from Ground Support Café.

Up from the floor before I can reach him,
in his seat, shoulders shaking.
Blood trickles down on periwinkle, but does not pour.

I press limp napkins into his hand, hold out the bottle.
I have no language left in me.
He turns his head away.

Ashamed, suddenly, of the smear of human stains
across the window,
I choke on my own uselessness.

A drowning boy does not cry out for water.
No one will stop this train.

**against cashmere**

cause i
fresh plucked from the oyster shell
all knitted and pearled
was left to lie

erased
no more or less defaced
than my backdrop
wearing his winey drool

pinkish droplets
spattering
my hand-wash-in-Woolite
block-dry-cashmere-white

beads of it
scattering
among the handsewn patterns
in the subway light

smelling the cashmere
matted yellow
against the urined floor

guilty of fashion

## Lady Ablaze

and in the gallery
amidst Magritte, Manet, and all
the women cluster
round no glowing faced Renoir
but to their knees do fall
and cast their gaze upon the wall
where is engraved
the ignited woman
called Lady Ablaze

and she for centuries
has paid in flames
for corpulence
for the muse, for the musings
burning from inside out
and not a flicker about
for her own dissipation

though the bedclothes drape unscathed
not even she would put her out
the lady ablaze

and in the gallery
the women see
and understand
not the genre, not the artist's hand
but the burning
the place where heat cannot escape
where first sparks flare and catch, unabated
under incendiary folds of them

the spontaneity
of human combustion

## Early Evening, Late September

You were just back from the war.
Your eyes were the color of coastal fog,
and you were lost in them.

Downstairs,
the aunts and uncles circled you,
anxious to hear news of the jungle, or of the desert.
So many battle landscapes,
who could know?

I took your hand,
and we climbed up to the roof, sat on the slope,
above the flaming trees, away from smothering embraces.
I asked if you would tell me, if you would try.
But your voice was low and level when you said
not yet.
And your eyes never left the horizon,
so I didn't ask again.

Not knowing yet
that the moment had already raced between us,
that you would be gone by Thanksgiving,
that my regrets
were already standing sentinel outside the door.

That there was only this,
this early evening, late September,
where the manes of sugar maples
tossed below us in the wind like the hair of women
who must have loved you long before,
before I loved you; before I failed to rescue,

before we sat there
on the slope line, cradling your homecoming
between us
like a broken, battered child.

## Garden of Air

My grandmother is tending her
                imaginary roses.
See how she moves, like a
                Kabuki dancer,
arms above her, pruning and shaping
                the thinnest air.

She takes my hand, this whisperer
                of roses,
leads me through the briar, pricks
                her bony finger
on some unseen thorny stem, but
                does not bleed.

She who has no memory or name for me
                keeps safe
a catalogue of every bloom.  The Floribunda,
                this one,
the Grandiflora. Guides my nose close to
                transparent Damask,

bouquet of Bourbon Rose.  Nods at the Seven Sisters,
                though I have never
seen them.  She plucks a living beetle from a
                Mother  of Pearl.
My grandmother is teaching me the art of
                invisible roses.

None smell so bitter, so sweet.  I break when she does sigh
                and linger
beside the Gallica, the oldest on the vine.
            Each day        I lose  more  of her
to this thieving garden of air.

Someday, I fear, this will all be mine.

## On the Line

We wait behind the yellow tape.
Our own arms wrap ourselves in the sticky heat,
as if we could insulate from the heresy of words like *active shooter.*
I think about the house of women who raised me.
Voices that blanketed me with "Hold back. Be patient. You're fine. No, you
really are fine. You require nothing".
Words that assault me now, in this place; stinging me, like a swarm of
yellow-jackets.

And then they are coming out of the school.
Hands over heads, in single file. Some of our children.
Everyone's children. Snaking in a grotesque conga line.
Inexplicably, I remember the footage of the camels in Libya.
3,000 camels herded in frantic lines from the Port of Tripoli
in artillery fire.
My son urging them on the screen: *Go faster! You need to go faster.*

And I see him then. Toward the end of the snake; not lost, but here.
One sleeve of the red shirt is torn and dangling.
It may be possible to mend it. From this distance I can't be sure.

I want to touch him. I want to lunge and break the yellow tape,
trample every living thing to get to him.
To shriek at that long line of women who wait with me, all the living
and the dead ones:
*No. Remove your hands from me.*
*This day, I will not wait my turn.*

## Gather Her Up Like Broken Branches

These times we're traveling
can slam our heads to the ground
pull our roots from the earth
dangle us like willows whipping
over turbulent streams

We are not unaware. We step out carefully.

We speak as we walk of the exhaustion of hummingbirds
the mantis swiveling its head from prayer to watch us
from the leaves
                      black smoke in Syrian skies
sun tea in jars
sweetened by August breeze

She touches my face now and again
to trace new shadows there
asks how it is with me

So we move on then
feet slipping sometimes at the water's edge
pulling each other always and forever back
as is the way with friends like these

I know she has fractured places in her
where the world can't see

I want to gather her up
                      like broken branches
before the winter freeze.

## Tea for One, in the Rabbit Hole
4-1-20

Today I ventured out in my paper mask
to my deserted café.
On the first day of April, the day of fools.

One scarred table has stayed behind,
one chair upended on top of it
belly up, legs in the air.

It is the table not worth saving:
the uneven one, the one that tilted,
spilling the latte foam.

Today, no matter. Today I will not be served.
I will sit on tilt alone.

Friends are scattered now. Bracing in place.
I picture them in hushed and hollow rooms,
face masks drawn, fingers latex-gloved;
eyes on cups in saucers, where liquid untouched cools.
Teatime in the age of cholera.

This is not Vietnam, I tell myself.
Boys hoisted home in body bags.
Not nine-eleven. Not the shuddering sweep of AIDS.

This is a pause. A mitigation.
A closure before reopening.
Search for a plateau, is what they say.

But, still, there is a biting breeze today
and I tighten my scarf against it.
Worries swirl and pile in heaps
against the café wall.

Back when we were knitted together,
we shared hibiscus tea
in a café on the Upper West Side.
You were in love again and flushed with expectancy.
I had finished a new poem and you wanted to hear it.
You had time, you said.

And so, we poured again from a white glazed teapot
etched with a drawing of Alice in Wonderland,
who looked unsettled and unnerved.

And the day tasted sweet like hibiscus and honey,
without the bitterness of loss or dread.

We drank it in, together on that day,
two fools convinced that everything bad had already happened.

## Sylvie

when we were eleven years
you danced for their pennies

your flesh already outgrowing your bones
your heart writhing, hidden beneath
the vastness of you
beneath the woman's breasts
that heaved and rolled above your other folds

the boys from the neighborhood
pitched coins at your feet
for your sad street corner rumba
dance, Sylvie      dance, Sylvie      dance
you were the sideshow, Sylvie
the carnival

i watched from my stoop
you crawl on pavement
to rake the filthy pennies
loose change in streetlight's glow

Sylvie, where you are, i hope you remember me
and do not forgive my failure

i who watched from the cheap seat
who paid no admission
who did not rise up to burn the tent down
stop the show
i who sat close enough to see
tears oozing up from the mountains of you
like a lava flow

## Beirut, baby

I see on the screen
the nurse who ran three miles from the blast in Beirut,
three premature babies against her breasts,
dangling from her as the hospital came down.
And I think of the will to run like that,
your arms full of new things, like tadpoles, wet things,
things not ready yet for the rocking of this world.
And I can't stop crying.
So I click away and now there is something new burning
in Syria, in Bosnia, Iraq or Pakistan, some gassing in some near or
far-off city, from air or ground.
And I am so damn tired, suddenly,
so I go outside, lie down in the green grass,
lower myself slowly
so as not to shake the ground, not to make tremble
what crawls and burrows underneath me:
the worms, the scarab beetles, white grubs and masked chafers,
the worker ants and queens;
to not disturb further the already strangling roots,
the soft bones buried there.
I stay there on my back, breathing hard, calves aching,
like I'd been running two, three miles
in no direction,
arms full of limbs still forming,
wild heart tapping code to each of them:
Better get ready, little one.
Everywhere you go from now on
it's gonna be Beirut, baby.
Explosives in your veins, all wired
and set to blow.

## Bring Your Dead to Me

Bring your dead to me.
Grief is so heavy and hard to carry;
you must unbend yourself,
unbow your head, unspeak their names for a while.

Bring your dead loves to me.
I will dance them for you for a night,
will wrap around my neck
the memory of their bones
and we will trip that light fantastic
across the varnished floor.

I will spin them, twirl them, guide them
glide them.
Will teach them the tango, cheek to cheek,
the waltz in perfect time, the mad fandango,
        while you are elsewhere, shoulders easing,
        breathing out and in.

And, oh, how we will dance the
Paso Doble:
bodies close, in binary rhythm,
chest and thighs held tight together.
I'll prop their heads up high,
keep bones from rattling
while I hear their histories.

And when you come to reclaim them,
        and you must, for I've no room
        to keep them, having my own, after all,
they will wear castanets on their fingers,
coins around their ankles,
and will hum home,
bells on their toes.

Trust me, tomorrow is another day for grieving.
Tonight,
bring all your dear and darling dead ones.
I crush the feet of the living,
but, oh the dead, how they do swing and sway.

## Orchids

turning back the eye
        i see your hothouse room
hyacinth and hibiscus
        heavy in the air
                everywhere
                    the aerosol of spring
            in excess hanging
                    clouds of sick perfume
turning back the eye
        i see you
camouflaged and couched
        in tropical bloom
            blinded by orchids
                words fallen petals
            between us
                in the hothouse room
      where
            heavy with hyacinth and loss
       you withered and i did not see
            never asking how it was with you

## Even So

I have flown out at myself
like startled pigeons
    like bats from under eaves
    in flashlight's glare

I have inched me
to the edge of icy cliffs
    forced my eyes
    to daggered rocks below

have crouched in shadows
waiting to step out
    and barricade my own way
    in the road
stretched me naked on the block
quivering under the blade

I have given the order in a foreign tongue
marched me into the gully
arms locked behind my head

even so
I've dragged me limp from riverbeds
    worked over me
pumping the careless heart
back to a rhythm it knows

stayed with myself
till first light
    humming lullabies
    only our ancestors have known

I have cursed both
the saved and the savior
    but clutched their hands at high tide
    even so

## What a Mother Must Know

nights will be fitful in this town
stretching out forever
under the sign that promises
"accommodations"

your child will grit her teeth in sleep
and wake with hollowed eye
refusing the air you offer her
clean between county lines

nothing will save her
not town fathers
the laying on of hands
this haven's sacred lore

and when you drift away
in the blistered dark
you dream it :
shoveling her under
with metallic rhythm
watching the small loaf
bake to crust
on the earthy floor

you'll wake and there it is
lodged in your throat
like a splintered swallow :

the air you came here for

**Visiting Hours**

I took you to the Vietnam Memorial once
to visit his name.
You could take flowers, I told you.
A calla lily, something small,
like a teardrop.
But you wanted your hands to be free.

By the time we had searched to find him
you were already stooped and shrunken
from the journey, his name so high on the wall, a stretch
for you.
Up on your toes, heels lifting out of sensible shoes,
you pressed your cheek against him,
hands spread across black granite.
Your blue veins, roadmaps to other sites
of other engraved boys.     Your reflection leaning in to rest her wet face
against your own.

Today I stand at the nursing home window,
watch you struggle alone for wind,
your hair rising up like wisps of white smoke
signaling a new pope, a crossing over.
I rest my face against the pane,
fingers stretching wide on the glass that is cool,
like skin.     I wait for your eyes to find me.     Your lips moving now,
you are reading my open palms.  Your name is recorded there.

## what have you got

what have you got to lose
when you are chasing the bus that swallowed her
with your arms full of peonies
their petals pulverized by wind
and you cannot outrun your future
with hands full of sorry stems
when one breast trembles
under the x-ray
bloated with dark shadows
and they say
take off the other for good measure
what have you got to lose
when you are frantic in solitude
mistaking it for loneliness
when you have emptied your pockets of faith
into the clanging cup of the faithless
when you are on the eighth floor
and flames have eaten the seventh floor
and you just need a minute
to feed from bare cupboard
this child's wild hunger
when they yell up
throw the bowl
and we will fill it
throw the child and we will catch it
what have you got then
what have you got to lose

## Not All Days Are Savage

My child lies sleepless down with loss tonight,
and I am out of the lie of lullabies.

What kind of mother tells her child:
not every day is merciful?
Some days we will trudge barefoot behind the hearse
to the funeral pyre, mercury in our veins.
Not every day brings beauty to disaster.
Some days guns glint in sunlight, bullets dance
across the avenues.
Some days tear towers down, leave smoking craters,
survivors draped in ash and bone.

Hush child, not all days are savage.
Some prepare us for asylum, usher us in
to taste what hunger is for.
Not every day brings forth a beast, nor requires an angel.
Some days wrench boot from throat
and startle us with tenderness.

Sleep now, one lid open,
for in the shifting shadows of peace and of terror
we move under the eyes of monstrous things.

What kind of mother knows such lullabies?
Enough of the bough that cracks and breaks, the mockingbird
that will not sing,
enough of the wolf's breath at the door.
I say instead: child, the heart sometimes is a wounded creature,
curled beneath the breast, not meant to be disturbed.
I will stay close, keep watch,
in case it stirs.

## Come Down Here

come down here
to the spattered synagogue
where the sidewalks are wet from weeping

Come. Down. Here.
rest your hands on broken desks in Newtown
too fragile to bear the weight of your fear

come down
with Mad Meg's army
marching past the corner where breath has no meaning
tell me the streets are not familiar here

look me in the face
tell me your eyes have no rivers
no fault line through your soul

tell me you cannot hear grief sharpen her blade
on stones very near

tell me again
how it cannot touch you
how it will not find you ever
never your door

leave this place then
whistle home through the dark park
whistle
whistle your way alone

## Hard Frost

the aging mother of my friend
her mind like tattered lace
wandered from her porch
in the savage winter
in her nightgown
and vanished into pitch dark air

for weeks my friend
took out his speckled dog
to sniff the fields and foothills
out through the cattails
       a blanket on his arm

hope is persistent
it seeps into the bloodstream
curls round the bones
and clings there
       it is all
       in a killing frost
       that keeps us warm

**Marks We Leave**

Chimpanzees of the Ivory Coast
will hoard
stockpiles of rocks
in hollows of trees.
                    Observers have seen them,
hunching forward
one by one,
choosing with care their rock from the hallowed cairn.
                    Such moments seek deliberation:
                    a jagged stone, perhaps, meant best for piercing,
                    or one worn round and smooth
                    as polished bone.
Then pacing backwards for a distance,
rock held long aloft,
before the guttural, half-human growl;
the hurling of it
against the bark
                    to mark the battered tree.

Primatologists puzzle it:
a game of sport here,
a sacred ritual,
a sweet release?

More like graffiti, then.
The aching rage of the vanishing.

No different
than the spray-painted howl we humans scrawl
                    on railway trestles
                    and abandoned walls,
before we disappear.

We will be soon gone,
but we were here.

## Two, In Isolation

I call you up to inquire about your state of being              in isolation
and you count out loud the number of beats              your heart

makes every minute and in what rhythm and pattern              and tune
And no you do not hear drums distant              banging slowly

and oh how can you be expected to hear the              chanting
when salons are shuttered against neglected locks      grown over your ears

You do not ask the extent of my horror or              the body count
and no you do not suffer hunger in isolation              does anyone really

As you are safe behind your blackout blinds              like that
no you have not seen streets drain and fill with pain              like a reservoir

When we sign off I wander to the yard              where the blind mole
has left his tell-tale mounded trail as he              burrowed through

I need to ask him right now where are              his roots
where has he come from and              is it of matter

How crushing how solitary was              the journey
Where will he go now and who is there to meet him      up ahead

Can he see to find his way there              after this

## Damage, done

after he'd told me of the hands that wrenched
and hurled him in the tender years,

I understood why he'd forgotten about the sun
rusting overhead, the shift-shaping of the moon

between waxing and waning, the wind singing
a cappella though a town, the blinking code of fireflies

after he'd unfurled the damage, so long folded,
I came to see why he cared not to water spring's

first green and hungry shoots, to wrestle poison
ivy from the strangling milkmaid roses

I know now why his fingers arched together like
a crumbling cathedral, and why his heart was

forever closed to the sanctuary of lost
and feral things

## Teaching to the Test

Today I am teaching my students their lessons
in survival.

We begin with the grammar of it:

Active: engaged in action, in a state of existence, an adjective:
to modify, describe the noun.
Shooter: (noun) A person who uses a gun on a particular occasion.
And now they know.

I show them how to camouflage faces with black Magic Marker.
Exposed skin reflects the light, draws the enemy's attention.
We want to disappear.

I tell them how to dig out shrapnel with a colored pencil, how to
move in zig zag patterns, how to drop, to roll.

We read about the history of Anne Frank, in the attic, becoming one with
silence.  We learn the math of sucking in our breath in darkness
and counting the seconds as we hold.

Last, we practice building forts, not out of sheets thrown over
clotheslines, blankets over chairs, but out of tiny desks turned
on their sides, tops facing the door.
How to curl behind them like small,
hunted creatures in the forest do.

I glance at the clock on the wall, that is merciful, that grants me
time for a lesson in French before they go.
Do we die tomorrow? a child asks, somewhere from a safe distance.
It must be enough only to pull down the mask and teach him, in this language
of love:
*On ne sait jamais.*
One can never know.

## Virus

In the winter of twenty-twenty
the virus, they insisted,
slithered through China,
    out from the wet markets
    into the heart of Wuhan
    and Hubei.
        Only ghosts rode the subway
        or walked the hutongs
        in Beijing.
In America,
we coughed into our sleeves,
scrubbed raw our fingers,
    recoiled within borders
    to accuse and sanitize.

But the virus, the other one,
was already with us.
Hatred
tunneling through air vents,
    exchanged in cold clouds
    on the avenues.
We passed it, ungloved,
in arenas
and on airwaves.
    Raised high
    our cups of steaming malice,
    shared them hand to hand; lips to lips.

And when abhorrence
pressed its filthy boot down
on human kindness,
    we drew in close,
    our mouths uncovered;
    breathed out the execrations
    and breathed them in.

Take off your face masks now.
They will do you no good.
If you have come this far,
you are already exposed.

## One More Sleep before the Wars

When you were still small enough
to lift,
your eyes half-lidded,
drunk from play,
I carried you in.

"Is there always a war?"
you whispered as you clung.

How to say
"Oh yes. Outside and within."

You are tall now,
back in your old room for a night, in a bed grown small.
Your breathing, deep.

How can you sleep
while the streets rage in Manhattan and Tehran,
the war horse pawing at the gates below?

I polish your battle boots by moonlight,
having nothing more to give you as you go.

Outside, the stars drop from the sky.
Piercing our windows as they fall.

I conjure every god I've never known
tonight
and mouth a wordless prayer to them all.

**Pérdida Insondable**

There is a name for every little thing:

*Kuchisabishii* tells us the Japanese
                        know what it is
to eat, not out of hunger, but for
                        the lonely mouth.

In Hebrew, *mizpah* is that
                braided thread
that binds us, when we are separated by distance or
                        by death.

*Lacuna*, from the Latin, to speak of
                        the blank space,
you will feel it,
                the missing part.

*L'appel du vide* is how the French come to warn us of
                        the impulse
for jumping from a higher place.  The call
                        of the void.

Where can we travel to find the Greek
                *kalopsia,*
and live in that delusion that things are
                        more beautiful
than they really are.

                Tell me, is there a word     that says
                to die for twenty dollars?

In Spanish, one word cannot hold it,
                two are required:
*pérdida insondable,*
unfathomable loss.

                There is a new language          to be learned now.
                Someone teach me, please,              the word
                for emptying and scouring          the streets,
                only to fill them again from          the same dark
                pool of sorrow.

## In the Dark, In the Deep

> *"I see the poets, who will write the songs of insurrection*
> *generations unborn will read or hear a century from now,*
> *words that make them wonder how we could have lived*
> *or died this way..."*   —Martin Espada

I speak from deep in the peat bog
under accumulated layers of deadened moss,
where acid centuries have turned my hair to red,
my face to bronze.

You will unroll us, mummified,
preserved along with the rotting noose and the poet's scroll,
peel back the membranes of a thousand years
of ire and disbelief.

So many bodies down here,
more than imagined or required,
the crimes against each other written in our flesh,
as in the wilting leaves of tea.

Here, where we are, folded in the peat and in the
soggy immortality,
let the acid do its work:
tan every face to the same dark chestnut;
each, many times murdered, not least by shame.

With deep respect to you, Espada,
how could we wonder how, when we did live like this,
that we would end this way?

## Every Once in a While You Want to Erase that Cardigan

In another time, Genesa, before they took you,
we were kids together, all our limbs sprawled
out on sand, sculpting palaces we would never
live in, and you were my dream catcher, my
sorrow-keeper, my nine-year-old sister queen,
and in the time after that, you would stare at
the photo I keep of you, where you wear a sweater
the shade of quicksand, your hands balled into fists on
your lap, face gutted and gobsmacked from stripped love
at seventeen,
hair Medusa-wild with braided serpents, eyes flown from the
lens, escaping to the back of your head,
and you would always say
*every once in a while I just want to erase that cardigan*
and we would say *oh yes someday*, laugh loud like teenage American queens,
but we lost time for that, Genesa, because at thirty-three you stepped
out into the street, hot from sweater and August air,
went strolling just to catch your breath, with your arms bare and
your swelling breasts and your long limbs and your earphones blaring
Aretha,
strolling out, hot, into the cool spray of bullets, without your cardigan,
like you owned the place, like you were a queen,
like you forgot that in another time you and I,
we planned to walk together on dead stones
in some exotic country, speaking a dead
language, dragging our guidebooks and
our children with us, and their children,
spitting in our tissues to wipe gelato
from their faces, while our crowns
of white hair blew apart
like dandelions in foreign breeze,
but you are my gone-sister now,
my golden statistic, bronzed
skin riddled with the bullets
of this time, lead in your
glorious veins, soundtrack of us
blasting Aretha, your wild hair
flowing red and undone
from these American streets,
to the sea.

## With the Red-Winged Blackbirds
*—in memory of George Floyd and all the others*

I am underneath the alder tree, watching
the red-winged blackbirds fall.

On the ground beside me is the book of
*Birds of North America,* open to the page

of glossy black and gleaming feathers, scarlet
shoulder patches, "theirs is an early, tumbling song".

Changes are coming, the book tells me, when you see
the red-winged blackbird.     He is the messenger of

a new awakening.   But nothing of this: birds tumbling
from cattails, from the willows and the alder, from the barbs of wire

and telephone lines.   I am paying attention now, to
all things, to the truth of matters.   I vibrate, shaken loose by so many

hovering chariots, swinging low. The book is silent.   Does not instruct
me how to step between the bodies, how to fold bent wings into a shroud.

The book is silent, and I am rocking, knees to breast,
endlessly rocking, watching dark rain fall.

As for the red-winged blackbirds, I will grow
hoarse and ancient trying to name them all.

**S**hellie **Harwood** is a poet, playwright, actress and teacher with a varied background in writing and theatre. She has taught Acting, Communication, and Poetry/Literature at universities, colleges and theatres in California, Idaho, Utah, Tennessee, and Connecticut. She has an MA in playwrighting, and has written several plays, including *Ember Days, Vicious Union,* and *Another Bite of the Moon.* Shellie has worked as an actress, performing throughout the country in regional and repertory theatres. She was born and raised in Idaho, but has spent much of her life moving about the country with her family. She is married, has one daughter, Morgan, and a son, Nicholas, both of whom are singers and performers.

Shellie has traveled throughout Europe, and lived and wrote for a year in Paris, France in 2017-18. She now lives in Connecticut with her husband, Allen, a calico, Katie, and golden doodle, Finnegan. "I love the dramatic snowstorms and the spectacular autumns in New England, but still find myself missing Paris. I had a profound "land memory" experience when I first arrived in Paris…as if I had lived there before, as if I was already a part of the place, somehow. And it is, of course, a writer's dream. Gertrude Stein said, 'America is my country, but Paris is my hometown.' I feel that…"

Writing has always been a passion for Shellie. She has written since she was very young, and has performed her work at readings and festivals, but it is only during the recent pandemic that she has begun to compile her poetry and distribute it for publication. Shellie's poems have recently been published in *Oberon, Mudfish 22, and Sixfold Poetry Summer 2020.* "I write every day, without fail. During the isolation and unease of the pandemic, writing has been my salvation."

Shellie has been awarded The Oberon Herbert Poetry Prize, established in honor of the revered Polish poet, Zbigniew Herbert. The award, for 2021, will be presented this fall by representatives of the Oberon Project and the Zbigniew Herbert Foundation of Warsaw.

This honor and cash award is presented to Ms. Harwood for her poem "With My Sister, in a Tornado Warning", for "displaying what Herbert considered essential: semantic transparency; using words as windows into emotions."

She is currently working on two books: one, a collection of pandemic poetry, the other, a full-length book of collected poems, "The Darkening."

www.ingramcontent.com/pod-product-compliance
Lightning Source LLC
La Vergne TN
LVHW090417070525
810591LV00007B/151